THE ART OF SELLING A DALLAS LUXURY

HOME

THE ULTIMATE GUIDE FOR HIGH-END PROPERTY OWNERS

KIM MELI LOVETT

The Art Of Selling A Dallas Luxury Home

The Ultimate Guide for High-End Property Owners

Adriel Publishing

FIRST EDITION

Printed in the U.S.A.

Cover design by Kim Meli Lovett

ISBN: 978-1-892324-98-6

www.KimLovettRealtor.com

Table of Contents

This comprehensive guide will help prospective luxury home sellers in the Dallas TX Metroplex navigate the complex world of real estate. With practical tips, real-life case studies, and expert advice, readers will gain the knowledge and confidence needed to master the sale of their luxury homes in one of the nation's most vibrant and competitive real estate markets. Whether you're a first-time seller or a seasoned investor, this book is your essential companion to achieving success in the luxury real estate market of Dallas.

Welcome to the Dallas, Texas Area Real Estate Market

In the heart of the Lone Star State lies a sprawling urban landscape that has captured the hearts and dreams of countless people seeking a place to call home. Welcome to the Dallas, Texas Metroplex Real Estate Market, a dynamic and ever-evolving landscape that offers a diverse array of opportunities for homeowners, investors, and enthusiasts alike. Here we will embark on a journey through this vibrant and exciting real estate market, exploring its unique character, historical roots, and the reasons why it continues to be a magnet for those seeking a prosperous and fulfilling life.

A City of Opportunities

The Dallas-Fort Worth Metroplex, often referred to simply as "DFW" or "The Metroplex," is one of the largest and fastest-growing metropolitan areas in the

United States. It is a wide-spanning region encompassing numerous cities and communities, including Dallas, Plano, Frisco, Rockwall and many others. With a combined population that ranks among the nation's largest, it is no wonder that the real estate market here is teeming with possibilities.

Historical Perspective

Dallas is a city steeped in history, its roots dating back to the mid-19th century when it served as a key trading post for settlers, cattle drivers, and railroad builders. The real estate market here has always been closely tied to the city's economic and cultural growth. Over the years, Dallas has evolved into a vibrant and diverse hub for commerce, education, technology, and culture, creating a rich and diverse tapestry of neighborhoods and communities that cater to people from all walks of life.

Economy and Employment

One of the driving forces behind the Dallas Metroplex's real estate market is its robust and diverse economy. The region is home to numerous Fortune 500 companies, including AT&T, ExxonMobil, and Texas Instruments. Its pro-

business environment, central location, and low tax rates have made it a hotbed for corporate headquarters and business expansion. This economic vibrancy ensures a steady influx of job opportunities, attracting a diverse workforce and subsequently driving the demand for real estate.

Residential Real Estate

Whether you're in the market for a luxurious suburban mansion or ranch, a trendy urban loft, or a charming historic home, the Dallas Metroplex has something for everyone. Its real estate market offers a wide range of housing options, and the region is known for its affordable cost of living compared to many other major metropolitan areas. This affordability, combined with strong job growth, makes it an attractive destination for both first-time homebuyers and seasoned real estate investors.

Commercial Real Estate

Dallas boasts a thriving commercial real estate market, featuring a mix of office space, industrial parks, and retail centers. The region's diverse business landscape and continued expansion have created a strong demand for commercial properties.

As companies continue to flock to the Metroplex, the opportunities for investment in this sector remain abundant.

Education and Culture

Dallas is home to a vibrant arts and culture scene, with world-class museums, theaters, and live music venues. The city also places a strong emphasis on education, with prestigious universities and colleges, including Southern Methodist University (SMU) and the University of Texas at Dallas, enhancing the area's appeal for students and academics.

Diversity and Inclusion

The Dallas area is known for its cultural diversity and inclusivity. Its neighborhoods reflect a rich tapestry of backgrounds, traditions, and communities, making it a place where individuals from all walks of life can find a sense of belonging.

Transportation and Infrastructure

Dallas boasts an extensive network of highways, a robust public transportation system, and a major international airport, making it a well-connected and accessible city. The region's commitment to infrastructure development ensures that residents and businesses can easily navigate the area.

The Future Awaits

As we dive deeper into the Dallas area real estate market, we will explore the distinct neighborhoods, housing trends, and the intricacies of buying, selling, or investing in this dynamic region. The opportunities are boundless, and the future holds great promise for those willing to seize them. In the chapters that follow, we will navigate the intricate world of the Dallas & surrounding area real estate market and help you discover the keys to success in this exciting and ever-evolving landscape. Welcome to a journey of opportunity, growth, and prosperity in the Dallas metroplex.

Why Luxury Home Sales in Dallas Matter

Dallas, Texas, is known for its thriving economy, diverse culture, and remarkable real estate market. Within this vibrant metropolis, the luxury real estate sector plays a crucial role, both as an indicator of economic health and a testament to the city's desirability. In this section, we explore the reasons why luxury home sales in the Dallas area matters, shedding light on the profound impact they have on the local economy, community, and the broader real estate landscape.

Economic Implications

One of the primary reasons luxury home sales matter in Dallas is the significant economic impact they bring to the region. Dallas has consistently been recognized as one of the fastest-growing cities in the

United States, and its robust economy is a major driver of luxury real estate sales. Here's why:

Job Creation: High-end residential properties contribute to job creation in the construction, interior design, landscaping, and property management industries. The construction of luxury homes often requires skilled labor and specialized materials, providing employment opportunities for local residents.

Property Tax Revenue: Luxury homes, with their higher valuations, generate substantial property tax revenue. These funds help finance essential public services, such as schools, infrastructure development, and public safety, benefiting the entire community.

Consumer Spending: Luxury homeowners tend to have higher disposable incomes, which stimulate the local economy through increased spending on goods and services, from fine dining and high-end retail to cultural and entertainment activities.

Attraction of Wealth: The presence of luxury homes in Dallas attracts high-net-worth individuals and successful entrepreneurs, encouraging them to invest in local businesses and contribute to the city's economic growth.

Cultural Significance

Luxury home sales are not just about economics. They also reflect the city's culture, history, and identity. The Dallas luxury real estate market has become synonymous with sophistication, elegance, and modern living. Here's why this cultural significance matters:

Architectural Heritage: Many luxury homes in the Dallas area are architectural marvels that showcase a range of styles from contemporary to historical. These properties contribute to the city's rich architectural heritage and serve as a source of pride for residents.

Neighborhood Aesthetics: The presence of luxury homes can enhance the overall aesthetics of a neighborhood, making it more appealing to both residents and visitors. This, in turn, can drive increased investment in local infrastructure and services.

Fostering Creativity: The process of designing and decorating luxury homes often involves collaboration with talented architects, interior designers, and artisans. This creative endeavor can have a ripple effect, inspiring innovation and artistic expression within the community.

Community Pride: Luxury homes contribute to a sense of community pride and identity, as residents take pride in their neighborhoods and the cultural cachet they bring.

Real Estate Landscape

The luxury home market in Dallas acts as a bellwether for the broader real estate landscape. Here's why it matters:

Price Trends: Luxury home sales often lead the way in price trends, serving as indicators of the overall health of the housing market. They can signal whether the market is cooling or heating up, providing valuable insights for investors and buyers at all price points.

Development and Innovation: The construction of luxury homes often introduces innovative building techniques, eco-friendly features, and cutting-edge technology. These innovations can eventually influence the design and development of more affordable homes.

Spillover Effect: High-end real estate development can lead to the revitalization of surrounding neighborhoods, increasing property values and improving amenities for all residents.

Luxury home sales in the Dallas area matter for various reasons, including their substantial economic impact, cultural significance, and influence on the broader real estate landscape. As Dallas continues to evolve as a dynamic and desirable city, the luxury real estate market will play a crucial role in shaping its future, reflecting the values and aspirations of its residents, and contributing to the city's overall prosperity and well-being.

Chapter 1
Understanding the Dallas Luxury Real Estate Market

Part One: The Dallas Metroplex – An Overview

As you explore the dynamic world of residential real estate in the United States, the Dallas metroplex stands out as a thriving hub of opportunities and diversity. Nestled in the heart of North Texas, the area encompasses a vast region that includes numerous cities, each with its unique character, amenities, and real estate market. This chapter will serve as your comprehensive guide to the residential real estate landscape in the Dallas & suburban areas, covering the key cities, neighborhoods, and factors to consider when investing in this dynamic region.

The Dallas Metroplex: A Booming Real Estate Market – Dallas is one of the fastest-growing metropolitan areas in the United States. With a robust economy, a diverse job market, and a high quality of life, it's no wonder that the metroplex has become a hotbed for residential real estate investment.

City Spotlight: Dallas

Dallas, is of course the largest city in the metroplex, offering a plethora of residential real estate options, from luxury high-rises in the Uptown district to historic homes in the charming neighborhoods of Lakewood and Highland Park. The city's diverse and vibrant culture, along with its strong job market, make it an attractive destination for those seeking urban living with a Texas twist.

The Suburbs: Plano, Frisco, and More

The suburbs of the Dallas are a testament to urban planning and development. Cities like Plano and Frisco have seen explosive growth in recent years, making them sought-after destinations for families and professionals alike. These communities offer a wide range of housing options, from contemporary townhomes to expansive suburban estates, all while maintaining a strong sense of community and excellent school districts.

Neighborhoods and Communities

Within each city and suburb, the metroplex features a diverse array of neighborhoods and communities, each with its own unique personality and lifestyle. From the historic charm of Bishop Arts District in Dallas to the family-friendly atmosphere of Allen, the residential landscape provides options for every taste and preference. Whether you're seeking a tight-knit community or an urban haven, you're sure to find a neighborhood that suits your needs.

Real Estate Trends

Understanding the current real estate trends in the area is crucial for any prospective homebuyer or investor. We will begin to explore the various factors that influence the market, including supply and demand, property values, and emerging hotspots, giving you the insight you need to make informed decisions.

Navigating the Real Estate Process

Purchasing a home in and around Dallas involves navigating a complex and ever-evolving market. From working with real estate agents to securing financing and understanding the legal aspects of a transaction, there are many steps in the residential real estate process, and even more details when it comes to luxury real estate.

Dallas is a real estate paradise, offering something for everyone. Its diverse cities, neighborhoods, and real estate market trends make it an exciting place to invest or find your dream home.

Part Two: Key Neighborhoods & Submarkets

In the sprawling metropolis of Dallas, Texas, the luxury real estate market offers a diverse range of neighborhoods and submarkets, each with its own distinctive character and appeal. As discerning buyers and investors explore the city's upscale properties, understanding the unique features of these key areas is essential for making informed decisions in this competitive market. Now we will delve into some of the most sought-after neighborhoods and submarkets that define luxury living in the Dallas area.

Highland Park

Often referred to as the "Beverly Hills of Dallas," Highland Park stands as one of the most prestigious and exclusive neighborhoods in the city. Nestled just north of Downtown Dallas, this area exudes a timeless charm with its tree-lined streets, grand estates, and meticulously manicured landscapes. Highland Park is known for its award-winning public schools, upscale shopping along Highland Park Village, and its close proximity to the Dallas Country Club. The luxury real estate market in Highland Park offers a mix of historic mansions and modern estates, making it a haven for affluent individuals seeking a blend of tradition and opulence.

Preston Hollow

Preston Hollow, located just north of Highland Park, is another upscale gem in the Dallas real estate landscape. This neighborhood is characterized by its grand estates, private gated communities, and the presence of some of the city's most prominent residents. From lushly landscaped properties to modern architectural marvels, Preston Hollow offers a wide variety of luxury homes. The area is also home to top-notch private schools and is known for its tranquility, making it an ideal choice for those seeking a serene, secluded lifestyle within the heart of the city.

Uptown and Victory Park

For those who are in search of the energy and vibrancy of urban living, Uptown and Victory Park are prime destinations in Dallas's luxury real estate market. These areas offer upscale condominiums, penthouses, and luxury apartments with stunning skyline views. Uptown's walkability, upscale dining, and proximity to arts and cultural attractions make it a favorite among professionals and young up-and-comers. Meanwhile, Victory Park, with its mix of residential, entertainment, and retail spaces, provides a more modern urban experience with convenient access to the American Airlines Center, home to the Dallas Mavericks and the Dallas Stars.

Turtle Creek and Oak Lawn

Turtle Creek and Oak Lawn, just west of Downtown Dallas, are renowned for their picturesque streets, mature trees, and elegant historic homes. The neighborhoods are adjacent to the scenic Turtle Creek and the Katy Trail, making them ideal for those who value green spaces and proximity to the arts district. Luxury condos with stunning views of the Dallas skyline are abundant in this area, catering to residents who appreciate the fusion of natural beauty and urban amenities.

Frisco and Plano

Moving north of the city, Frisco and Plano have emerged as rapidly growing luxury real estate submarkets. These suburbs are characterized by their spacious homes, exceptional public schools, and family-friendly environments. The Stonebriar Country Club, Legacy West, and The Star, where the Dallas Cowboys practice, are key attractions in these areas, adding to their appeal for luxury buyers seeking a balance of space and convenience.

Southlake and Westlake

To the west of Dallas, Southlake and Westlake are prime destinations for those looking for an opulent lifestyle. These suburbs offer exclusive gated communities, estate homes, and excellent public and private schools. With easy access to the Dallas/Fort Worth International Airport and a range of upscale shopping and dining options, Southlake and

Westlake cater to affluent individuals seeking a tranquil yet convenient living environment.

Rockwall County

Nestled amid the lush meadows and along the serene shores of Lake Ray Hubbard, lies the beautiful county of Rockwall. Known for its scenic beauty and a rich historical heritage, Rockwall County has emerged as a sought-after destination for those seeking the epitome of luxury living in the Lone Star State. The county's luxury real estate market has been on an exciting trajectory, offering a unique blend of modern amenities, natural beauty, and small-town charm.

Part Three: Market Trends & Dynamics

The Dallas real estate market has long been a focal point for investors, homeowners, and real estate professionals alike, as Dallas has consistently demonstrated resilience and growth. In this section, we will probe into the market trends and dynamics that define the real estate landscape in the Dallas area.

Market Overview

Dallas has experienced significant growth over the past few decades. As the population has steadily increased, the demand for real estate has also surged. The city's job market is a primary driver of this growth, with a wide range of industries, including technology, healthcare, finance, and energy, contributing to a strong and diversified employment base.

Housing Market Trends

The Dallas housing market has remained relatively affordable compared to other major metropolitan areas. This affordability, combined with the state's lack of income tax, has attracted many new residents to the area. While there have been periodic fluctuations, the general trend has been one of appreciation. The COVID-19 pandemic brought about a temporary slowdown, but the market quickly rebounded, and home values continued to rise.

Supply and Demand

The supply and demand dynamics in the Dallas area are noteworthy. The demand for housing is consistently strong due to the city's growth, while the supply of new homes has struggled to keep pace. This has led to a competitive market with multiple offers on properties, often resulting in bidding wars.

New Developments

New residential developments are continually emerging in and around Dallas. Suburban areas like Frisco, McKinney, and Plano have seen substantial growth as people seek a balance between urban amenities and more spacious living. Additionally, downtown Dallas has witnessed a revitalization, with a surge in new condominiums and mixed-use developments.

Commercial Real Estate

Office Space

Dallas boasts a robust commercial real estate market. The city is a corporate hub, with many major corporations headquartered in the area. It's no secret that COVID-19 has accelerated trends toward remote work, leading to a reevaluation of office space requirements. However, Dallas remains an attractive destination for companies looking to establish a physical presence.

Retail and Mixed-Use

Retail and mixed-use developments have continued to flourish, driven by the city's growing population and economic stability. Areas like the Dallas Design District and the Bishop Arts District have gained prominence, offering a unique blend of shops, dining, and residential spaces.

Investment Opportunities

The Dallas area presents a variety of investment opportunities in both residential and commercial real estate. As the population continues to grow, the demand for rental properties remains strong. Investors are drawn to Dallas's favorable rental market conditions, including the potential for cash flow and long-term appreciation.

Financing

Financing options are readily available in Dallas, with a range of lenders offering competitive rates and terms. Additionally, the Texas real estate market benefits from a stable regulatory environment, which provides a sense of security to investors and lenders alike.

Challenges and Future Trends

Despite the numerous advantages of the Dallas real estate market, there are certainly challenges and future trends to consider:

Infrastructure and Traffic: As the population continues to grow, the infrastructure and transportation systems must adapt to accommodate increased traffic and urban development.

Property Taxes: Rising property taxes are a concern for homeowners, and this issue is closely monitored by both residents and potential buyers.

Environmental Considerations: Sustainability and eco-friendly real estate developments are becoming more critical as environmental concerns gain prominence.

Impact of Remote Work: The extent to which remote work becomes a permanent feature of the job market could impact the demand for office space.

Part Four: Competitive Analysis

The Dallas area has seen substantial growth and development, making it a hotspot for luxury real estate. With its strong economy, diverse job market, and an appealing quality of life, many affluent individuals are drawn to this vibrant city. As a result, the luxury home market in the Dallas area has become increasingly competitive. In this article, we will conduct a competitive analysis of the luxury home market in the Dallas, TX area, exploring the key factors that define this market and the trends shaping its future.

Market Overview

The Dallas area luxury home market is characterized by a wide range of opulent properties, each offering an array of features and amenities. Luxury homes in this market are typically defined by their size, quality of construction, exceptional finishes, and upscale features. These homes often boast impressive architecture, spacious interiors, state-of-the-art technology, and meticulously landscaped grounds.

Competitive Factors

Location: Location remains one of the most significant factors influencing the luxury home market in the Dallas area. Prestigious neighborhoods such as Highland Park, University Park, Preston Hollow, and Southlake continue to attract high-net-worth individuals due to their proximity to excellent schools, cultural amenities, and convenient access to the city's financial and business districts.

Amenities and Features: Luxury buyers in Dallas demand the best of the best. Features like home theaters, wine cellars, outdoor entertainment spaces, smart home automation, and spa-like master suites are becoming the norm. Homes with features such as private gyms, swimming pools, and lush gardens tend to command higher prices.

Market Trends: One notable trend in the Dallas luxury home market is the demand for eco-friendly and energy-efficient features. Sustainable building materials, energy-efficient appliances, and solar panels are increasingly appealing to luxury homebuyers looking to reduce their environmental footprint and energy costs.

New Construction vs. Historic Properties: Buyers in this market often face a choice between new construction and historic properties. New construction offers modern amenities and the latest in design, while historic homes provide character and charm that is more challenging to come by with newer builds. The demand for historic properties has been rising, with discerning buyers willing to invest in extensive renovations to preserve the heritage of their homes.

Local and Global Influences: Dallas's luxury real estate market is influenced by both local and global factors. Local economic conditions, employment opportunities, and population growth play a substantial role. Additionally, global influences, such as the international buyers looking for investment opportunities, can impact market dynamics and trends.

Market Players: Several real estate agencies and luxury homebuilders dominate the Dallas area luxury home market. These firms specialize in catering to the unique needs of high-end clientele, offering tailored services and extensive networks to connect buyers with their dream homes.

Future Outlook: The future of the area luxury home market looks promising. With continued economic growth and increasing demand from affluent individuals and families, the market is expected to remain thriving. As the city continues to evolve and urbanize, new luxury developments are likely to emerge, offering a mix of contemporary design and prime locations.

However, external factors, such as economic downturns or changes in tax policy, can influence the luxury market's performance. Buyers and sellers should always stay informed about market conditions and seek professional advice to make informed decisions.

Chapter 2: Preparing Your Luxury Home for Sale

Part One: Evaluating Your Property

Selling a luxury home is not just a real estate transaction; it's a sophisticated and intricate process that requires careful planning and preparation. To ensure a successful sale at the highest possible price, it's essential to evaluate your luxury property thoroughly and make it as attractive as possible to potential buyers. In this chapter, I'll guide you through the process of evaluating your luxury home and getting it ready to sell.

Start with a Home Inspection

The first step in evaluating your luxury home is to have a professional home inspection conducted. This will help you identify any hidden issues that might affect the sale. As you probably know, high-end buyers often demand top-notch quality, so addressing any structural, mechanical, or cosmetic problems is crucial.

Enhance Curb Appeal

First impressions matter, and that's why enhancing the curb appeal of your home is essential. Make sure the exterior of your property is well-maintained. This includes landscaping, cleaning driveways and walkways, and giving your home a fresh coat of paint if needed. Consider hiring a professional landscaper or a stager to ensure your property makes a stunning first impression.

Declutter and Depersonalize

Luxury home buyers typically seek a blank canvas that they can personalize to their taste. Remove personal items, family photos, and clutter from your home to help potential buyers visualize their future living space. That doesn't mean you have to completely revamp the style of our home, it simply means let the beauty speak for itself. This will also make your property appear more spacious and inviting.

Luxury properties often benefit from professional staging services. A professional stager can help highlight your home's best features, showcase its potential, and create a luxurious atmosphere that appeals to discerning buyers. Staging may include rearranging furniture, adding stylish decor, and selecting sophisticated color schemes. Stagers can offer a multitude of suggestions on how to make spaces in your home stand out.

Repairs and Upgrades

Identify any necessary repairs and consider making strategic upgrades to increase the value of your property. This could involve updating the kitchen, bathrooms, or even adding some more lavish features such as a wine cellar, a home theater, or a state-of-the-art security system. Consulting with a real estate agent to determine which improvements will yield the best return on investment, can be very helpful.

Highlight Unique Features

Once prospective buyers step through the threshold of your home, they should be greeted by a sense of luxury, comfort, and exclusivity. Here are some key considerations:

Neutral Color Palette: A neutral color scheme allows buyers to envision their personal style within a space. Subtle tones like soft grays, creamy whites, and warm creams can create an elegant backdrop for luxurious furnishings.

Furniture Selection: High-quality furniture is a must in luxury homes. The pieces should complement the architecture of the space and reflect a cohesive design theme. Artfully arranged furniture can define functional areas and flow within the home.

Art and Accessories: Fine art, sculptures, and carefully chosen accessories can add personality and style to the space. They should be thoughtfully placed to enhance the overall ambiance.

Lighting: Appropriate lighting is essential to showcase the property. Incorporate a combination of ambient, task, and accent lighting to create a sense of drama and comfort. Remember that when a potential buyer walks into a room, their eye will be more attracted to light and bright.

Scent and Atmosphere: A pleasant and inviting scent can leave a lasting impression. High-end candles or essential oil diffusers can infuse the home with an appealing aroma, and soft background music can set the mood. When choosing a scent for your home, it's wise not to go with something overwhelming or perfumy. A nice light citrus scent is always a good choice. And if music will be playing during an exclusive open house or private showing, make sure the volume only serves as background and is something instrumental.

The Importance of Detail

Every detail counts when staging a luxury home. Pay close attention to cleanliness, organization, and the elimination of a lot of "stuff." Buyers should be able to visualize the property as a pristine and comfortable space that they could call home, and if a space feels too filled, it can give more of a chaotic impression.

Part Three: Pricing Strategies

Selling a luxury home is an endeavor all its own, that requires careful consideration and a well-thought-out approach. One of the most critical aspects of this process is determining the right price. The importance of pricing strategies when placing a luxury home for sale cannot be overstated. Luxury real estate presents a distinct set of challenges and opportunities that demand a tailored pricing strategy to ensure a successful and profitable sale.

Understanding the Luxury Real Estate Market

Before delving into the significance of pricing strategies for luxury homes, it's crucial to grasp the unique dynamics of the market. Luxury properties are not just houses; they are lifestyle investments. Potential buyers in this market are often discerning, sophisticated, and seeking not only a home but also an exclusive living experience. As such, pricing luxury homes is not as straightforward as it is for standard residential properties.

The Importance of the Right Price

Attracting Qualified Buyers: Luxury homes are typically characterized by their premium features, exceptional craftsmanship, and unique locations. As a seller, you want to attract potential buyers who can genuinely afford and appreciate these qualities. Pricing your home correctly is essential to bring in qualified buyers who are serious about making a purchase. Overpricing may seem attractive, especially in a competitive market. However I would caution you to fight the urge to over-price, it can deter genuine buyers and can leave your home sitting on the market longer than it should. On the other side of the pricing coin, underpricing may raise suspicion or even worse, leave money on the table.

Maximizing Return on Investment: Luxury home-owners often expect a significant return on their investment. Pricing your luxury property accurately ensures that you receive a fair market value, if not more, for your home. Strategic pricing can also help you optimize your profit while maintaining a competitive edge.

Reducing Time on Market: Time is a critical factor in the luxury real estate market. A home that stays on the market for an extended time can be both financially and emotionally draining for sellers. A well-thought-out pricing strategy can help you sell your property in a reasonable time frame, minimizing the inconvenience of constant showings and maintaining the allure of exclusivity.

Comparative Market Analysis (CMA): A CMA involves analyzing recent sales of similar luxury properties in your area. This method provides valuable insights into current market conditions and allows you to benchmark your property against similar listings. While CMA's in luxury areas can be a bit tricky due to the uniqueness and special amenities that each property holds, an experienced real estate agent with expertise in luxury homes can help you conduct a comprehensive CMA. This will prove to be a very valuable tool that is needed to determine a winning price for your home.

Appraisal by a Professional: Obtaining an independent appraisal from a certified appraiser can provide an objective and accurate assessment of your home's value. This is especially helpful when dealing with luxury properties that may not have direct comparables in the market. Getting an independent appraisal down prior to putting a home on the market will also give insight into what they buyer's appraiser will be looking at, and provide a map for comparison.

Consider Seasonality: The luxury real estate market, like any other, can experience seasonal fluctuations. Timing your listing to coincide with peak buying seasons can influence pricing and market demand. A knowledgeable real estate professional can advise you on the optimal timing for your specific location and property. It's well-know that the fourth quarter is typically a slower real estate time, that's not to say that it's not an ideal time to get your property prepped for a sale, and have a realtor create a marketing plan.

Stay Informed: Market conditions are subject to change, and it's essential to stay informed about local, national, and global economic factors that might affect the luxury real estate market. Flexibility in your pricing strategy may be necessary to adapt to evolving market dynamics.

Part Four: Working With Professionals

Selling a luxury home is often not for the faint of heart! It requires a specialized approach to ensure optimum success. While some homeowners may consider handling the sale themselves to save on commission fees, there are compelling reasons why working with a professional realtor is invaluable in the luxury real estate market. I will explore the importance of partnering with a seasoned realtor when selling your high-end property in this section.

Market Expertise

One of the primary benefits of working with a professional realtor in the sale of a luxury home is their in-depth knowledge of the local real estate market. Sure you can do the homework yourself, but all of research on the internet can't compare to real world experience. Realtors are intimately familiar with the unique scenarios of the luxury segment, including pricing trends, neighborhood specifics, and current market conditions. Their expertise allows them to accurately assess the value of your property, maximizing your chances of securing the best possible sale price. Their role is significant and the time that they will put in to sell your home is invaluable. I may be a bit biased on this subject, but working with a pro can be the difference between a luxury property that sells, and one that either sits on the market for months, or eventually sells for much lower than it could have.

Access to Exclusive Networks

Realtors have access to exclusive networks and contacts within the industry that are not readily available to the general public. These connections include other high-net-worth clients, potential buyers, and fellow real estate professionals. Leveraging these networks can lead to faster sales and opportunities that might not be achievable through private sales.

Marketing and Presentation

The presentation of a luxury property is crucial to attracting discerning buyers. Realtors have the skills and resources to market your home effectively. This includes professional photography, virtual tours, broker open houses to showcase the property, and the creation of high-quality marketing materials. They can also recommend staging professionals to ensure your home is presented in the best possible light, which can significantly increase its appeal to potential buyers.

Negotiation Expertise

Selling a luxury property often involves complex negotiations. Realtors are trained and experienced in handling these intricate transactions, and they can help you secure the most favorable terms and conditions. They act as intermediaries, skillfully managing the give-and-take between parties to achieve a win-win outcome, and of course your realtor is working for your best interests. They are your advocate, spokesperson, and negotiator.

Time and Stress Management

Selling any home can be a time-consuming and stressful process, especially if you attempt to do it on your own. Professional realtors can take on the bulk of the work, allowing you to focus on your other responsibilities and enjoy peace of mind. They handle everything from scheduling showings and open houses to managing offers/negotiations and the closing process.

Contractual Expertise

Real estate transactions often involve intricate contracts that must be navigated carefully. Realtors are well-versed in these aspects, ensuring that all contracts are sound and protecting your interests throughout the sale.

Price Optimization

Setting the right price for a luxury property is a delicate balance. Overpricing as we discussed, can deter potential buyers, while underpricing can mean losing out on your property's true value. Realtors use their market knowledge and experience to determine the optimal pricing strategy, maximizing your return on investment.

Confidentiality and Privacy

Luxury homeowners often value their privacy. Professional realtors understand the importance of discretion and can implement strategies to protect your anonymity and security during the sale process.

Chapter 3:
Marketing Your Luxury Home

Part One: Building Your Marketing Plan

Selling a luxury home demands a strategic and tailored approach to marketing. The high-end real estate market is characterized by unique challenges and a discerning clientele. To successfully sell a luxury property, you must create a comprehensive marketing plan that not only showcases the property's features but also conveys the lifestyle and exclusivity associated with it.

Understand The Target Audience

Prior to creating a marketing plan, it's crucial to understand the potential buyers. Luxury home buyers are often looking for more than just a place to live; they seek an aspirational lifestyle. Consider factors such as their demographics, interests, and motivations. Are they international investors, wealthy entrepreneurs, or successful families seeking a primary residence? Tailoring marketing efforts to cater to their desires will yield best results.

Highlighting Unique Selling Points

Identify and emphasize the distinctive features of the luxury home. This may include architectural elements, exclusive amenities, breathtaking views, or historical significance. High-quality photography, 3D virtual tours, aerial photographs, and professional staging can help showcase these aspects effectively. It's essential to create a compelling narrative around the property that goes beyond the physical attributes and appeals to the emotions of potential buyers. Emotions and desirable presentation are at the heart of every sale.

Establish an Online Presence

In the digital age, an online presence is paramount for marketing luxury homes. A well-designed, user-friendly website dedicated to the property is a must. Ensuring that it includes high-resolution images, detailed descriptions, and, if possible, a virtual tour are musts. Leveraging social media platforms to showcase the property, and well designed creative marketing initiatives increase visibility and showing performance.

Utilize Video Marketing

Video is a powerful tool in luxury home marketing. Creating professional video tours of the property, showcases its grandeur and luxury. These videos can be shared on social media, the website, email marketing, and video-sharing platforms like YouTube. Aerial drone footage, in particular, can provide a breathtaking view of the property's surroundings.

Collaborate with Influencers and Luxury Brands

Teaming up with influencers and luxury brands can add credibility to marketing efforts. Invite prominent individuals from the local community or luxury lifestyle influencers to visit and promote the property. Additionally, partnerships with luxury brands like high-end furniture stores, art galleries, or automotive companies can enhance the perceived value of the home.

Host Exclusive Events

Organizing exclusive events, like private viewings, broker open houses with sips and bites, cocktail parties, or art exhibitions at the property, can attract high-net-worth individuals and generate buzz. These events provide an opportunity for potential buyers to experience the property in a social setting, enhancing their emotional connection with it.

Targeted Advertising

In luxury real estate marketing, targeted advertising is key. Utilizing both online and offline advertising methods, including paid search ads, social media ads, and high-end real estate magazines are all strong strategies. Using refined demographic targeting to reach individuals who match the ideal buyer profile can also prove to be very useful.

Foster Relationships with Luxury Real Estate Agents

Luxury real estate agents often have access to a network of affluent buyers. Working with a realtor promotes collaboration with other established agents who specialize in luxury properties and provides more opportunities for your home to be seen.

Part Two: Digital & Traditional Marketing

In the world of luxury real estate, the process of selling a high-end home requires a delicate balance of traditional and digital marketing strategies. While the core principles of real estate marketing remain consistent across the board, the luxury market demands a more tailored and exclusive approach.

The Fusion of Traditional and Digital Marketing

Luxury homes represent a niche market, where the value is often in the details and the intangibles. To effectively market such properties, real estate professionals must seamlessly blend traditional and digital marketing techniques. This fusion of strategies allows for a comprehensive and compelling approach that captures the attention of potential buyers and stands out in a competitive market.

Traditional Marketing: Timeless and Elegant

Traditional marketing methods have not lost their charm when it comes to luxury real estate. The tactful use of these strategies can add a touch of timeless elegance to the marketing campaign for a luxury home. Here are a few key components of traditional marketing in this context:

High-Quality Print Materials: Luxury homes deserve high-quality brochures, pamphlets, handouts, and print advertisements. These materials should be meticulously designed, using professional photography along with well-crafted copy to showcase the property's unique features, amenities and architecture.

Exclusive Open Houses: Exclusive, by-invitation-only open houses can create a sense of exclusivity and allure. By carefully curating the guest list and ensuring a high level of personal attention, these events allow potential buyers to experience the property in a unique and intimate setting.

Relationship Building: Building personal relationships with potential buyers is often a cornerstone of traditional luxury real estate marketing. Agents may host private dinners, attend exclusive events, or network within elite circles to connect with high-net-worth individuals.

Digital Marketing: The Stage For A Global Audience

Digital marketing is indispensable in today's real estate landscape, including the luxury market. It allows for broader reach, data-driven insights, and engagement with a global audience. Here are some digital marketing strategies that can elevate the marketing of luxury homes:

High-End Property Websites: Creating a dedicated website for the luxury property is essential. These websites should be aesthetically pleasing, intuitive, and provide a comprehensive virtual tour of the home. Professional videos, 3D walkthroughs, and interactive floor plans can help potential buyers immerse themselves in the property.

Search Engine Optimization (SEO): Optimizing online content and website structure for search engines is crucial for making the property visible to potential buyers. By targeting relevant keywords, luxury real estate agents can attract organic traffic from individuals seeking high-end properties.

Social Media Marketing: Luxury properties benefit from a strong presence on social media platforms. Instagram, in particular, is a visual medium that allows for stunning photo and video content. Content should be carefully curated to convey the lifestyle associated with the property.

Email Marketing: Email campaigns can be personalized and used to nurture relationships with potential buyers. Sending regular updates, exclusive content, and property insights can help maintain engagement and interest.

Integration is Key

The most successful marketing strategies for luxury real estate seamlessly integrate traditional and digital techniques. For example, hosting a private, exclusive open house can be coupled with live streaming on social media platforms to allow a global audience to participate virtually. The print materials distributed at the event can include QR codes that lead to the dedicated property website.

In the world of luxury real estate, it is essential to understand that no two properties are the same. The marketing strategy should be customized to the uniqueness of the home, the preferences of potential buyers, and the current market conditions. By fusing the best of traditional and digital marketing, real estate professionals can ensure that they not only reach their target audience but also create a lasting impression that aligns with the exclusivity and grandeur of luxury homes.

Part Three: Targeting Luxury Buyers

In the world of luxury real estate, the sale of a high-end property requires a unique approach. Luxury homes are not just places to live; they are status symbols, investments, and lifestyle statements. As such, the art of targeting luxury buyers demands a careful and strategic effort. In this chapter, we'll explore the key principles and strategies for identifying and reaching the most discerning and affluent individuals in the real estate market.

Understanding the Luxury Buyer Persona

Before diving into the intricacies of targeting luxury buyers, it's crucial to understand the luxury buyer persona. Luxury buyers are a distinctive segment of the real estate market. They often possess a high net worth, sophisticated tastes, and a desire for exclusivity. However, luxury buyers are not a homogenous group, and it's essential to differentiate between various subgroups within this niche market.

High Net Worth Individuals (HNWIs): These individuals typically have a net worth well into the millions or even billions of dollars. They seek luxury properties not only as homes but as investments and status symbols. They are driven by a desire for exclusivity and are often willing to pay a premium for unique features and locations.

CEOs and Entrepreneurs: Successful business leaders and entrepreneurs are often attracted to luxury homes due to their busy and demanding lifestyles. They seek comfort, privacy, and amenities that cater to their professional and personal needs.

Celebrities and High-Profile Individuals: Celebrities, athletes, and other high-profile individuals require homes that offer security, privacy, and extravagance. They are often motivated by the need to escape the public eye.

International Buyers: Luxury real estate often attracts international buyers seeking a safe haven for their wealth, a second home, or a place to conduct business. Understanding the specific motivations, preferences, and lifestyles of these luxury buyer personas is the foundation of effective targeting.

Tailoring Your Marketing Approach

Once you've identified your target luxury buyer persona, it's time to tailor your marketing approach. Luxury buyers are discerning, and they expect a level of service and presentation that matches the grandeur of the properties they seek.

High-Quality Photography and Videography: Invest in professional photography and videography to showcase the property's finest features. Aerial shots, 3D tours, and well-composed images are essential to creating a captivating visual presentation.

Exclusivity and Discretion: Luxury buyers often value privacy above all else. Emphasize the property's exclusivity and your commitment to discretion in your marketing materials.

Leverage Technology: Utilize advanced technology like virtual reality tours, augmented reality apps, and AI-driven chatbots to provide potential buyers with an immersive and convenient experience.

Personalized Relationships

The sale of a luxury home often hinges on the strength of personal relationships. Luxury buyers may require a higher level of trust and confidence in the agent or brokerage representing the property. Personalized, concierge-level service is key.

Private Viewings: Arrange private viewings to accommodate the schedules and preferences of the luxury buyers. This demonstrates your commitment to their needs.

Concierge Services: Offering concierge services that go beyond the purchase itself. This could include introductions to local amenities, schools, or service providers to make the transition to the new home as seamless as possible.

Luxury Networking: Leveraging a network of high-net-worth individuals and connections in the luxury industry to attract potential buyers. Attending high-profile events and cultivating relationships within exclusive circles.

In targeting luxury buyers, it's crucial to remember that the luxury market is dynamic and ever-evolving. Stay attuned to market trends, changing buyer preferences, and emerging technologies to maintain your competitive edge in the world of luxury real estate. In the end, the art of targeting luxury buyers is about delivering an unparalleled experience that matches the prestige of the properties you represent.

Part Four: The Power of Professional Photography

In the world of real estate, the power of first impressions cannot be overstated. When it comes to selling luxury market homes, the impact of those initial moments can be the difference between a quick sale at the desired price and a property languishing on the market. In an era where visual content is king, professional photography emerges as a formidable tool in the arsenal of real estate agents and sellers alike.

The Visual Symphony

Before a potential buyer even sets foot inside a luxury home, they embark on a journey through a visual symphony of images. The old adage "a picture is worth a thousand words" has never rung truer in the realm of real estate. The exquisite details, the sweeping vistas, the lavish interiors—all of these must be conveyed eloquently and enticingly through visuals alone. Professional photographers possess the skill and artistry to orchestrate this symphony, ensuring that every note played captures the essence of luxury living.

The lens through which a professional photographer views a luxury property is akin to that of a master painter contemplating a blank canvas. They understand the interplay of light and shadow, the importance of composition, and the necessity of highlighting architectural features that define opulence. A well-chosen, well-placed shot can elevate a seemingly ordinary room into an opulent sanctuary.

Eliciting Emotional Responses

When selling luxury real estate, it's not just about listing features and specifications; it's about creating an emotional connection with the potential buyer. Professional photography is the bridge that conveys the emotions a property can evoke. The golden hues of a luxurious sunset casting a warm glow over a private pool, the elegant symmetry of a grand staircase, or the gentle play of light on marble countertops—all of these elements have the power to elicit emotions of desire, aspiration, and longing.

Luxury buyers often seek not just a house, but an experience, a lifestyle, and a statement of their own success. Through carefully curated images, professional photographers can transport viewers into the world of refined living, allowing them to envision themselves in that environment. The emotional pull of such images can be irresistible.

Setting the Stage for Exclusivity

A luxury home is not just a dwelling; it's an enclave of exclusivity and distinction. Professional photography can establish this sense of privilege from the very first glance. It's not merely about showing what a property has to offer; it's about crafting a narrative around it. The visual story told by professional photographers can make a property stand out as a unique and highly desirable asset.

In the world of luxury real estate, the adage "you get what you pay for" holds true for professional photography. Cutting corners in this department can not only undermine the perceived value of a property but also deter potential buyers. Conversely, investing in professional photography sends a clear signal to prospective clients that you recognize the intrinsic value of what you're selling.

The Art of Presentation

The art of selling luxury homes is a multifaceted endeavor, and professional photography is an essential brushstroke on the canvas of presentation. It not only enhances the visual allure of a property but also amplifies its intrinsic value. In the realm of luxury real estate, where discerning buyers expect nothing less than the best, professional photography is not just a luxury—it's a necessity. By working with skilled photographers who understand the nuances of your market and your property, you're not merely showcasing a house; you're unveiling a lifestyle, an aspiration, and a dream. In the next chapter, we'll delve deeper into the strategies for finding and collaborating with the right professional photographers to maximize your success in the luxury real estate market.

Chapter 4: Navigating the Sales Process

Part One: The Important Role of a Realtor

We've touched on this before, however in the world of luxury real estate, the role of a realtor cannot be overstated. Selling a luxury home requires a specialized set of skills, knowledge, and experience. From marketing to negotiation and beyond, a seasoned realtor is the linchpin in the successful sale of high-end properties.

The Gatekeeper of Luxury

Luxury homes are not simply real estate transactions; they are expressions of opulence, lifestyle, and prestige. Potential buyers of luxury homes are knowledgeable and have done their homework, and they often expect a level of service and attention commensurate with the property they are considering. This is where a realtor's role takes center stage. A luxury real estate agent acts as the gatekeeper to this exclusive world, connecting buyers and sellers while facilitating an experience that goes beyond the ordinary.

Expertise in Market Dynamics

Understanding the intricacies of the luxury real estate market is no small feat. Realtors who specialize in this niche sector have an in-depth knowledge of local and international market trends, neighborhood values, and the specific factors that influence high-end home sales. Whether it's the current state of the economy, the impact of geopolitical events, or the latest design and architectural trends, a proficient realtor possesses a wealth of knowledge that is invaluable to both buyers and sellers.

Effective Marketing and Exposure

Selling a luxury home is not about merely listing it on the Multiple Listing Service (MLS), crossing your fingers, and hoping for the best. It demands a comprehensive and tailored marketing strategy that reaches a targeted audience. Realtors in the luxury market employ a range of marketing tactics, from professional photography and videography to virtual reality tours, high-end brochures, and exclusive events. They understand the power of discretion and privacy and know how to leverage both to attract the right buyers while respecting the seller's wishes.

Negotiation and Problem-Solving Skills

In the luxury real estate world, negotiation takes on a whole new level of complexity. Realtors must navigate intricate deals with high net worth individuals, often involving complex financial structures, proof of adequate funds to purchase the home, and unique contingencies. An experienced luxury realtor is not only an expert negotiator but also a skilled problem solver, capable of finding creative solutions to overcome any obstacles that may arise during the transaction. Their success equals your success, and realtors in this realm of real estate sales value the importance of that.

Global Connections and Networks

Luxury home buyers often hail from various parts of the world, making it essential for realtors to have a broad network and international connections. These connections can be a significant asset when trying to match a luxury property with the right buyer, whether they are located locally or across the globe. A well-connected realtor can tap into a vast pool of potential buyers, giving a luxury home the best chance to find its perfect owner.

Preserving Privacy and Confidentiality

Luxury homeowners often prioritize privacy above all else. A trusted luxury realtor understands the need for discretion and maintains the highest levels of confidentiality throughout the sales process. This level of professionalism not only protects the seller's interests but also ensures a seamless and respectful experience for all parties involved.

In the world of luxury real estate, a realtor is not just a representative; they are a trusted advisor, a marketing expert, and a problem solver. They bring to the table a vast set of skills and experiences that are essential for navigating the intricacies of the luxury market. When selling a luxury home, the role of a realtor is not just important–it's vital. In the pages that follow, we will delve deeper into the specific tasks and responsibilities that make a luxury realtor indispensable in the world of high-end real estate.

Part Two: Negotiation Strategies

Selling a luxury home is an art form, requiring a honed set of negotiation strategies to cater to a discerning clientele. We are going to delve into the nuanced world of luxury real estate negotiations, examining the strategies employed by successful agents and the principles that guide these transactions.

Understanding the Luxury Home Market

Before we can discuss negotiation strategies, it's essential to comprehend the nature of the luxury home market. Luxury homes are not just properties; they are a statement of prestige. Buyers in this segment are not merely looking for a place to live; they seek exclusivity, and a clear reflection of their success. This understanding is the foundation upon which effective negotiation strategies are built.

1. Tailored Approach

One size fits all doesn't work in luxury real estate. Each property has its own story, as do the buyers interested in it. A tailored approach to negotiation is paramount. This begins with conducting thorough market research to understand the specific property's value and its uniqueness. This knowledge empowers agents to position the property effectively, addressing the buyer's desires and highlighting what makes it a rare gem.

2. Building Relationships

Luxury real estate is all about cultivating strategic relationships. Successful agents build trust, not only with their clients but also with other agents and key players in the industry. These relationships often open doors to off-market properties, exclusive listings, and potential buyers that may not be readily available in the public domain.

3. Patience and Discretion

The luxury home market moves at a different pace. High-net-worth individuals often take their time to make decisions, and transactions may stretch over an extended period. Agents must exercise patience and discretion, respecting the privacy and preferences of their clients. Understanding when to push and when to step back is an art form in itself.

It's also imperative that sellers exercise patience. While we may have gotten used to multiple offers, and quick closings, the luxury real estate market has it's own personality that doesn't conform to overall real estate trends.

4. Price Realism

While luxury properties command high price tags, it's crucial to ensure that the asking price is realistic and supported by market data. Overpricing a luxury home can again, deter potential buyers, and it may linger on the market for longer than desirable. Effective negotiation includes guiding sellers toward a competitive yet reasonable pricing strategy. Of course we all like to believe that our properties should yield top dollar, and keeping an open mind where price is concerned is essential to a successful sale. Not taking a price recommendation as an insult, but as trusted advice is important.

5. Storytelling

Luxury homes often have a vibrant story to tell – a history, an architectural masterpiece, or attractive features. Effective agents use storytelling to create an emotional connection between the property and potential buyers. They narrate the history, the lifestyle, and the future possibilities that come with owning such a distinctive property.

6. Staging and Presentation

Presentation is key in luxury real estate. Agents often make the invest in high-quality staging and professional photography to showcase the property's best features. The art of presentation extends to property showings, where agents curate the experience to leave a lasting impression on potential buyers.

7. Negotiating Value, Not Just Price

When working on the sale of an estate, negotiation goes beyond haggling over price. It's about negotiating the value of the property, the lifestyle it offers, and the intangible benefits that come with it. Successful agents are adept at highlighting these aspects and showcasing them as part of the overall package.

In the world of luxury home sales, the negotiation table is not just a place for give and take; it's a stage where art, the story, and relationships converge to create exceptional real estate transactions. By understanding the unique dynamics of the luxury market and embracing these tailored strategies, real estate agents can excel in the art of selling luxury homes.

Part Three: Handling Offers & Counteroffers

The negotiation process is often a very delicate dance. Selling a luxury market home is not just about price, it encompasses so much more. We'll explore the art of handling offers and counteroffers to ensure a successful sale in the high-end market.

Setting the Stage

Before we dive into the negotiation process, it's essential to have a solid understanding of the current market conditions and all that sets a certain property apart from others for sale in the area. Pricing, well laid out plans, and a marketing structure all critical components.

Receiving the First Offer

When the first offer arrives, it's an exciting moment for all. The offer might be from a serious buyer who sees the true value in your property or simply a starting point for further negotiation. Here's how to handle this crucial juncture:

Review the Offer Carefully: Sit down with your real estate agent and carefully review the offer. Pay close attention to the offered price, contingencies, financial ability, requested option time, and any special requests.

Evaluate the Buyer: Understand the buyer's motivation. Are they financially qualified to close the deal? Do they have a genuine interest in the property, or is this just one of many offers they're making?

Consult with Your Real Estate Agent: Your agent's expertise is invaluable at this stage. They will guide you through the offer and help you decide whether to accept, reject, or counter it.

Counteroffer Strategy

In the luxury real estate market, it's not uncommon to enter into a counteroffer negotiation. When formulating your counteroffer, consider the following tips:

Focus on the Big Picture: While price is important, don't let it be the sole focus. Emphasize the all aspects of what your property offers. Highlight any upgrades or customizations that add value.

Negotiate Tactfully: Be prepared for some back-and-forth. Diplomacy is key. Avoid coming across as too aggressive, as it can discourage potential buyers. While it's important to stand firm on items that are important to you, on those of lesser importance have some flexibility. No one likes to feel as though there is no give and take at play.

Request Pre-Approval: A pre-approval is a must for those who are using financing as opposed to a cash purchase. It's difficult to take an offer seriously without appropriate and valid financial backing attached to it.

Consider Incentives: If the price is non-negotiable, explore other incentives such as covering closing costs, paying for title and a extensive home warranty or including high-end furnishings in the deal.

Set a Deadline: Ensure the negotiation process doesn't drag on indefinitely. Set a reasonable deadline for the buyer to respond to your counteroffer.

Handling Multiple Offers

Multiple offers certainly are common, especially with highly desirable properties that are priced effectively. This can create a sense of urgency and competition among potential buyers. Here's how to navigate this situation:

Inform All Parties: Let all interested parties know that multiple offers are on the table. Transparency is essential, and it can also help drive up bids.

Evaluate Each Offer: Compare the terms and conditions of each offer, not just the price. Consider the buyer's financial strength, contingencies, and closing timelines.

Leverage the Offers: If possible, use the presence of multiple offers to your advantage during negotiations. You can encourage buyers to put their best offers forward.

Consider Backup Offers: In case the primary offer falls through, having a backup offer in place can save time and keep the momentum going.

Part Four: Contracts & Legal Considerations

Unlike standard residential transactions, luxury homes often come with higher stakes, larger sums of money, and a more discerning clientele. Let's take a look at the essential contracts and aspects involved in selling a luxury market home.

The Listing Agreement: Setting the Stage

Before a luxury home can be officially offered on the market, the homeowner must enter into a listing agreement with a real estate agent or brokerage. This agreement sets the terms and conditions of the relationship, including the agent's responsibilities, the duration of the agreement, the asking price, and the agent's commission.

Given the substantial sums involved, it's vital for luxury homeowners to carefully review the listing agreement. Attorneys who specialize in real estate can provide valuable insight, helping ensure that the contract serves the best interests of the seller.

Property Disclosures: Transparency is Always Best

Full disclosure is essential. Sellers are typically required to provide comprehensive information about the property, including any known defects or issues that might affect its value or desirability. Failure to disclose relevant information can lead to legal complications, including potential lawsuits.

Luxury homeowners should work closely with their real estate agents and legal advisors to ensure that all necessary disclosures are made. This includes but is not limited to issues related to the property's structure, past renovations, environmental concerns, and any legal encumbrances like easements or restrictive covenants.

Due Diligence and Inspections: Protecting Your Investment

Luxury home buyers often conduct extensive due diligence, including thorough property inspections and research. Sellers should anticipate that the buyer will request inspections covering all aspects of the property, from the foundation to the roof, and may even include specialized inspections, such as for wine cellars, swimming pools, or state-of-the-art security systems.

It's crucial for sellers to cooperate with the inspection process and ensure that the property is well-prepared for scrutiny. It may seem daunting to go through a series of inspections, however not doing so, or questioning why a buyer wants them done can appear as if the seller has something to hide. Failing to address potential issues can lead to renegotiations or even the termination of the sale.

Closing: Crossing the Finish Line

As the sale approaches closing, sellers must carefully review all closing documents, ensuring that the terms and conditions align with the agreements made during negotiations. Title searches and insurance are paramount to verify the property's clear title and to safeguard against any unforeseen claims.

Closing is the final step in the sale of a luxury home, and it requires precision and thoroughness. Legal advisors play a crucial role in ensuring that all aspects of the transaction are in order and that the seller's interests are protected.

Contracts and legal considerations are pivotal to a successful sale. Sellers must work with experienced professionals, including real estate agents and attorneys who specialize in luxury transactions, to navigate the intricacies and safeguard their investment. With proper legal guidance, sellers can confidently navigate the process and maximize the return on their luxury property.

Chapter 5:
Showcasing Your Home to Potential Buyers

Part One: Hosting Open Houses

The open house is a crucial element in the marketing strategy for selling high-end properties. A well-executed open house, whether it be tailored to brokers or buyers, can be the difference between a swift sale at the desired price and a property languishing on the market for an extended period. In this chapter, we will explore the key strategies and best practices for hosting open houses that cater to the unique needs and expectations of luxury homebuyers.

Setting the Stage

Before the doors swing open to welcome potential buyers, it's essential to ensure a home is in pristine condition. Here are some steps to set the stage for a successful open house:

a. Professional Staging: Consider hiring a professional stager who specializes in luxury homes. They can help highlight the property's best features and create an ambiance that resonates with potential buyers.

b. Deep Cleaning: A spotless home is non-negotiable in the luxury market. Invest in a thorough cleaning, paying attention to every detail, from gleaming countertops to immaculate floors.

c. Minor Repairs: Fix any minor issues, such as leaky faucets, loose doorknobs, or cracked tiles. These details matter to discerning buyers.

d. Curb Appeal: First impressions are paramount. Ensure the exterior of the property is well-maintained and attractive, from the landscaping to the front entrance.

Timing and Promotion

Choosing the right date and promoting the open house effectively are critical steps in attracting the right audience:

a. Timing: Luxury homebuyers often have busy schedules. Consider hosting open houses on weekends or in the late afternoon to accommodate their needs. In regard to broker open houses, your real estate agent typically will opt to do a lunch time or early evening event, including light bites and cocktails.

b. Online Presence: Utilize high-quality photography, virtual tours, and drone footage to showcase the property online. Leverage social media platforms, luxury real estate websites, and email marketing to reach potential buyers.

c. Exclusive Invitations: Send personalized invitations to affluent individuals, real estate agents, and potential buyers who may be interested in the property. Hosting private, invitation-only events can create an air of exclusivity and help boost attendance.

Security and Privacy

Security is a significant concern when showcasing luxury homes. To ensure the safety and privacy of the property and its occupants, take the following precautions:

a. Professional Security: Hire experienced security personnel to manage access to the property during the open house. They can also provide assistance with crowd control and ensure a smooth experience for visitors.

b. Secure Valuables: Remove valuable items and personal belongings from the property before the open house to prevent theft or damage.

c. Non-Disclosure Agreements: Consider having attendees sign non-disclosure agreements to protect sensitive information about the property and its owners.

Luxury Amenities

Highlight the unique features and amenities of the luxury home to captivate potential buyers:

a. Property Tour: Provide guided tours of the property to showcase its best features, from spacious master suites to cutting-edge home theaters and impressive outdoor spaces.

b. Wine and Hors d'oeuvres: Offer a selection of fine wines and gourmet hors d'oeuvres to create a luxurious and welcoming atmosphere for your guests.

c. Concierge Services: Consider offering concierge services during the open house, such as valet parking or private transportation for attendees.

Engaging with Potential Buyers

During the open house, your realtor will with potential buyers and answer their questions. Provide information on the neighborhood, local amenities, and the lifestyle the property can offer. Listen to their feedback and adjust your approach accordingly.

Part Two: Private Showings

In the world of luxury real estate, the selling process is not just about showcasing a property; it's about crafting an unforgettable experience. Private showings play a pivotal role in this process, offering an exclusive glimpse into the lifestyle that a potential buyer could enjoy within the confines of a luxurious home. In this chapter, we will explore the art of conducting private showings when selling a luxury market home.

The Essence of Luxury Showings

When dealing with high-end properties, the objective of a private showing is not simply to display the home's features and amenities but to convey a lifestyle, an image, and an atmosphere that resonates with the prospective buyer. Private showings are a carefully choreographed performance that combines the physical elements of the property with the emotional elements of storytelling.

Creating the Perfect Setting

Preparing a luxury property for a private showing is a meticulous process. The home must be in pristine condition, with every detail accounted for. It should feel inviting and welcoming from the moment a potential buyer steps through the front door. This means ensuring that all surfaces are immaculate, that the property is well-staged, and that the ambiance is set to perfection. Lighting, scents, and even music can all contribute to the creation of an enchanting atmosphere.

The Power of Personalization

In the luxury market, one size does not fit all. Every private showing should be tailored to the specific interests and preferences of the potential buyer. Luxury real estate agents must invest time in understanding the individual's needs, desires, and dreams. Knowing whether they have a penchant for wine cellars, a passion for home theaters, or an affinity for sprawling gardens is essential. This personalization allows the agent to highlight the property's most appealing aspects, thereby connecting the dots between the property and the buyer's aspirations.

Exclusive Access and Discretion

One of the hallmarks of a luxury property showing is exclusivity. Potential buyers in this market expect a sense of privilege, and that means granting them exclusive access to the property at a time that suits their schedule. This not only enhances the feeling of exclusivity but also allows the buyer to explore the property without feeling rushed or crowded. Discretion is paramount, too. Luxury buyers often value their privacy, and real estate agents must be respectful of this by maintaining a discreet and confidential approach.

Storytelling Through Experience

The most effective luxury showings are not just about pointing out features but about crafting a narrative. Luxury real estate agents become masterful storytellers, weaving a tale of the property's history, its unique architectural features, and the lifestyle it can offer. They help potential buyers envision their own story within the walls of the home, creating an emotional connection that is often the key to a successful sale.

Building Relationships

In the luxury real estate market, relationships are everything. Private showings provide an opportunity for real estate agents to build a personal connection with potential buyers. These interactions are not just transactional; they are the foundation of trust and rapport. In the luxury market, buyers often turn to agents who understand them, their tastes, and their aspirations.

Part Three: Highlighting Unique Features

While the fundamentals of real estate marketing remain consistent, the luxury market presents its own set of challenges and opportunities. To excel in this niche, it is crucial to recognize and emphasize the special features and qualities that make a luxury property truly exceptional.

Luxury market homes, by definition, are a cut above the rest. They are not just places to live but rather expressions of a lifestyle, status, and personal taste. Buyers in this market aren't merely seeking a place to hang their hat; they are searching for an experience, a refuge, and a reflection of their success. Therefore, highlighting the unique features of a luxury home becomes paramount in the selling process.

Exclusivity and Privacy: In the luxury real estate market, privacy is a highly sought-after feature. Many high-net-worth individuals value seclusion and exclusivity. Whether it's a secluded estate surrounded by lush landscaping or a penthouse with discreet access, these unique features should be prominently featured in your marketing materials.

Architectural Excellence: Luxury homes often boast architectural designs that are nothing short of breathtaking. Unique and innovative designs, the use of high-end materials, and exceptional craftsmanship can be showcased through professional photography, virtual tours, and videos. Buyers in the luxury market appreciate the artistry and the investment in such details.

High-End Amenities: Luxury properties typically come with an array of high-end amenities, from spa-like bathrooms and gourmet kitchens to home theaters, wine cellars, and expansive outdoor living spaces. Ensure that these amenities are not just mentioned but highlighted with vivid descriptions and visuals.

Location and Views: Location is a paramount factor in luxury real estate, and the views from the property can be an absolute game-changer. Oceanfront homes, properties with panoramic cityscapes, and homes nestled in pristine natural settings offer an unmatched experience. Emphasize the unique selling proposition that the location and views provide.

Smart Home Technology: Many luxury homes are equipped with the latest smart home technology, offering convenience, security, and energy efficiency. Highlight these advanced features that make life in the property more comfortable and secure.

Historical Significance: Some luxury properties have historical significance, which adds to their allure. If the property has an interesting past, sharing its historical value can create a deeper emotional connection with potential buyers.

Customization and Personalization: The luxury market often welcomes customization and personalization. Buyers are drawn to homes that can be tailored to their preferences. Emphasize the potential for customization and any unique features that have been customized for the current owner.

Landscaping and Outdoor Spaces: Beautifully landscaped gardens, courtyards, pools, and outdoor kitchens can transform a luxury property into a private oasis. Capture these elements in your marketing materials, as they contribute significantly to the overall appeal.

Security and Privacy Features: Security is a top concern for luxury homeowners. Mention and showcase the state-of-the-art security systems and privacy measures in place to provide peace of mind to potential buyers.

Sustainability and Energy Efficiency: In today's luxury market, sustainability and energy efficiency are increasingly important. If the property features green technology, LEED certification, or other sustainability credentials, make sure to highlight them.

In the luxury real estate market, it's not just about selling a house; it's about selling a lifestyle. By skillfully accentuating the unique features and qualities that make a luxury property stand out, you can connect with discerning buyers on a deeper level and ultimately, close deals more effectively. In the chapters that follow, we'll delve deeper into the strategies and techniques for effectively marketing luxury homes and maximizing their value in a competitive market.

Part Four: Creating a Memorable Experience

Showcasing a high-end property is not just about providing a tour; it's about creating an emotional connection that leaves a lasting impression.

Before your prospective buyers even arrive, meticulous planning and preparation are essential. A successful showing starts with setting the stage, and this begins long before the actual tour.

1. Pre-Show Prep

The first step is ensuring the property is in impeccable condition. Luxury buyers expect perfection, so any signs of wear and tear must be addressed. Hire professional cleaners, stagers, and repair specialists to ensure that every aspect of the property is in pristine condition.

2. Curb Appeal

The first impression is often the most important. Invest in landscaping and exterior lighting to create a captivating entrance. A well-maintained garden and a grand entrance can captivate potential buyers from the moment they step out of their car.

3. Tailored Marketing

Craft a tailored marketing plan for the property, including high-quality photography and video tours. Highlight the unique features, amenities, and lifestyle that the home offers. Ensure that your marketing materials evoke an emotional connection and a sense of exclusivity.

Personal Touches That Make a Difference

Once your potential buyers step through the front door, it's time to immerse them in a world of luxury. Create a customized and memorable tour that goes beyond simply showcasing rooms and features.

1. Concierge Service

Begin the showing with a warm and personalized welcome. Offer a concierge service that takes care of the buyers' needs, whether it's a beverage, a light snack, or assistance with coats and bags.

2. The Story Sparks Interest

Narrate the story of the property. Discuss its history, unique architectural elements, and the lifestyle it can provide. Allow potential buyers to envision themselves living in the home, entertaining guests, and enjoying the amenities.

3. Personalized Touches

Tailor the tour to the specific interests and preferences of each buyer. If they're wine enthusiasts, focus on the wine cellar or cellar-like spaces. If they have a passion for gourmet cooking, highlight the kitchen's high-end appliances and layout.

4. Sensory Experiences

Engage all the senses. Play soft, soothing music in the background, create a pleasant aroma using scented candles or diffusers, and ensure the lighting sets the right mood in each room.

Unforgettable Amenities

Luxury homes often come with a range of amenities that can truly set them apart. Make sure to showcase these amenities effectively during the tour.

1. Spa-Like Retreats

Highlight luxurious bathrooms with spa-like features, including steam showers, soaking tubs, and heated floors. Allow potential buyers to experience a sense of relaxation and escape.

2. Outdoor Paradise

If the property has an expansive outdoor space, focus on creating a seamless indoor-outdoor experience. Open up doors and windows to show how the living space flows into the garden, pool, or terrace.

3. Technology Integration

Emphasize the smart home features, from integrated sound systems to security and lighting controls. Showcase how technology can enhance convenience and luxury.

4. Entertainer's Dream

If the property is built for entertaining, create a memorable experience by showcasing areas like a home theater, a bar, or a grand dining room. Paint a picture of the lavish parties and gatherings that the space can host.

Follow-Up and Feedback

The showing doesn't end when potential buyers walk out the door. After the tour, maintain the connection with personalized follow-up, showing appreciation for their time and answering any questions promptly. Seek feedback to continuously improve your showings and adapt to buyer preferences.

Creating a memorable experience during luxury home showings requires attention to detail, personalization, and a commitment to making each visit special. By focusing on the emotional connection and the unique features of the property, you'll leave a lasting impression and increase your chances of a successful sale in the competitive luxury market.

Chapter 6: Closing the Deal

Part One: The Inspection & Appraisal Process

Inspections and appraisals are critical aspects of the transaction that ensure both the buyer and seller make informed decisions. We're going to discuss the essential elements of the inspection and appraisal process for luxury market homes, highlighting their significance and providing guidance to navigate this crucial phase.

The Importance of Inspection and Appraisal

Setting Up For Success: The inspection and appraisal process sets the stage for a successful sale by providing objective insights into the property's condition and its fair market value. For luxury market homes, where prices can run into millions and comparable properties can be challenging, these processes are even more crucial.

Negotiation Leverage: Sellers can use the results of the inspection and appraisal to their advantage, as it provides a clear picture of the property's strengths and any areas that may require attention or improvement. Conversely, buyers can use these findings as leverage in negotiations.

Risk Mitigation: For both parties, the inspection minimizes the risk of unforeseen issues post-sale. It can uncover hidden problems that, if undisclosed, could lead to legal complications or damage the property's reputation.

The Inspection Process

For luxury homes, hiring a certified and reputable home inspector is paramount. Luxury properties often have many specialized features and advanced systems that require specialized expertise.

Thorough Examination: The inspector will thoroughly examine the property, inside and out. They will assess the structural integrity, electrical, plumbing, HVAC systems, and any other critical components. For luxury homes, specialized inspections, such as for swimming pools, wine cellars, or extensive landscaping, may be required.

Detailed Report: The inspector will provide a detailed report, highlighting any issues, both minor and major. Sellers can choose to address these issues before listing, thus potentially increasing the property's value. Alternatively, they can adjust the asking price accordingly.

Legal Requirements: Luxury market homes may be subject to additional legal requirements, such as environmental impact assessments or historical property evaluations. Ensure you are well-versed in local regulations.

The Appraisal Process

An appraiser experienced in luxury properties is crucial. They will assess the home's value, taking into account its unique features, location, and current market conditions.

Comparative Market Analysis: Appraisers use a Comparative Market Analysis (CMA) to evaluate the property's worth. This involves comparing it to similar luxury homes that have recently sold in the area. As mentioned before, this can be a tricky task. Homes in the high-end sector can't simply be evaluated by square feet and proximity, there are many features that distinguish them from other homes in the area.

Consideration of Features: Luxury properties often come with exclusive features like high-end appliances, custom finishes, or extensive acreage. These factors are taken into account during the appraisal.

Documentation: The appraiser will document their findings in a comprehensive report. For sellers, this report can serve as a strong selling point, while for buyers, it helps in ensuring they are making an informed investment.

Navigating Challenges

Challenges for Sellers: Luxury homes may have unique features that can be challenging to appraise accurately. To address this, provide documentation of any custom improvements or features that add value to the property.

Challenges for Buyers: For buyers, it's essential to carefully review the inspection and appraisal reports to understand the property's condition and fair market value fully. This information is vital when negotiating the purchase price.

Part Two: Preparing for Closing

As the journey to selling a luxury market home nears its final destination, it's time for the seller to focus on the intricate and essential details leading up to the closing. I will guide you through the crucial steps to ensure a smooth and successful closing process.

1. Final Walkthrough

Before the closing date is set, it's essential to schedule a final walkthrough with the buyer. This is an opportunity to ensure that the property is in the same condition as when the purchase agreement was made. Pay attention to any agreed-upon repairs or improvements and ensure they have been completed to the buyer's satisfaction.

2. Clean and Stage

Your luxury home should be in impeccable condition for the final walkthrough and the closing. Consider hiring a professional cleaning service to make sure every corner sparkles. Staging is also crucial at this stage. Fresh flowers, tasteful décor, and proper lighting can make a world of difference when the buyers walk through your home for the last time.

3. Gather Documents

Compile all the necessary documents related to the property. This includes:

- ✓ Deed to the property
- ✓ Mortgage documents
- ✓ Title insurance policy
- ✓ Homeowner's association documents
- ✓ Property tax records
- ✓ Inspection reports
- ✓ Any warranties or guarantees
- ✓ Any relevant permits or licenses

Having these documents readily available will expedite the closing process and build the buyer's confidence in their purchase.

4. Communicate with Your Real Estate Agent

Stay in close contact with your real estate agent. They will guide you through the closing process, keep you informed of any updates, and ensure that all the necessary paperwork is in order. Your agent's experience and expertise will be invaluable during this critical phase.

5. Address Legal and Financial Matters

Before the closing date, consult with your attorney and financial advisor. Ensure all legal and financial obligations are met. This includes paying off the remaining balance of your mortgage, settling any outstanding liens or judgments, and addressing any potential tax implications.

6. Secure Your Belongings

As the closing date approaches, start packing and securing your personal belongings. This will make the transition smoother and ensure that your home is ready for its new owners. Consider hiring professional movers to assist with the process, especially for larger luxury properties.

7. Pre-Closing Inspection

Shortly before the closing, the buyer may want to perform one last inspection. Be accommodating and ensure that the property is accessible for this purpose. The pre-closing inspection is an opportunity for the buyer to verify that the property is in the expected condition.

8. Be Prepared for Closing Costs

Closing costs can vary, but sellers typically incur expenses such as real estate agent commissions, transfer taxes, and other fees associated with the sale. Consult with your real estate agent or attorney to understand what costs you'll be responsible for and prepare for these expenses.

9. Closing Day

On the day of closing, gather all relevant parties, including the buyer, seller, real estate agents, and attorneys, at the designated location. Be prepared to sign the necessary documents and transfer the title of the property to the buyer. Once all documents are signed and funds are exchanged, the property officially changes hands.

10. Celebrate and Move On

Once the closing is complete, congratulate yourself on a successful sale. It's time to let go and move on to your next adventure. Be sure to leave a welcome letter for the new homeowners, offering them any insights or tips about the property or the local area, and wish them well in their new luxury home.

Closing a luxury market home is a process that requires meticulous attention to detail and expert guidance. By following these steps, you'll be well-prepared for a seamless closing, ensuring a successful transition to the new owners and the next chapter in your life.

Part Three: Overcoming Common Hurdles

As a luxury home seller, you've navigated the intricate dance of staging, marketing, and negotiations to finally arrive at the threshold of closing the sale. However, there are still hurdles to clear before you can hand over the keys to your prized property. In this chapter, we'll explore some of the most common challenges luxury home sellers face and how to overcome them, ensuring a smooth and successful closing.

Inspection Issues

Once you have a buyer, inspections are an inevitable part of the process. Luxury homes often have intricate systems, custom finishes, and unique features, which can lead to potential inspection issues. To overcome this hurdle, consider having a pre-inspection done before listing your property. This can help you identify and address any issues in advance, reducing the likelihood of surprises during the buyer's inspection. Make necessary repairs and provide documentation for the maintenance and history of your home to reassure the buyer and their inspector.

Financing Challenges

In the luxury real estate market, it's not uncommon for buyers to use various financing options, including jumbo loans, which come with stricter requirements. A hurdle that can emerge is the buyer's ability to secure financing, especially if they need approval for a substantial loan amount. To mitigate this risk, work with a buyer's agent who specializes in luxury properties and can help pre-qualify potential buyers. Additionally, consider offering financing contingencies in your contract, ensuring that the buyer has a clear path to securing the necessary funds.

Legal and Title Issues

Luxury homes often come with more complex legal and title considerations, such as easements, restrictive covenants, and homeowner's association rules. To overcome this hurdle, it's crucial to conduct a thorough title search and work with a real estate attorney who specializes in high-value transactions. Address any title issues promptly and ensure all necessary documents are in order, so there are no surprises during the closing process.

Emotional Attachments

Selling a luxury home can be an emotional journey, especially if it has been a cherished family property. Overcoming the emotional hurdle may require a shift in perspective. Try to detach yourself emotionally from the property and focus on the end goal, which is a successful sale. Stay open to negotiations and be willing to compromise where necessary, all while keeping in mind the greater financial benefits of the sale.

Timing and Contingencies

Timing is a critical element in luxury real estate. Buyers may have specific timing needs, whether related to relocating, school schedules, or other factors. Overcoming timing hurdles may involve being flexible with your closing date or considering contingency clauses in the contract. Work closely with your real estate agent to find creative solutions that accommodate both your needs and the buyer's.

Closing the sale of a luxury home can be a complex and sometimes challenging process. However, with careful planning, market knowledge, and the support of experienced professionals, you can navigate these common hurdles and ensure a successful sale that leaves both you and the buyer satisfied. In the next chapter, we'll delve into the closing process and the final steps in transferring ownership of your luxury property.

You've made it to the closing table and it's almost time to celebrate!

Funding and Financial Arrangements: The title companies escrow agent will be in touch throughout the entire closing process. As it nears the end, they will make sure that you receive applicable statements, and instructions for funds to be transferred to your account. Make sure to review all title documents thoroughly with your agent and legal counsel to ensure that everything is in place to your satisfaction.

Final Walkthrough: Final walkthroughs typically happen in the last few days before closing. The buyer may opt to do this with simply their real estate agent, or perhaps with an inspector just to make sure all things are in order.

Utilities and Services: In the final two weeks prior to closing, make sure that all utilities and other services are aware of the closing date and if you want them to be transferred or shut-off when that date comes.

Closing Costs: The title company will send you the closing statement/disclosure. This will outline payoffs to any outstanding mortgages, real estate agent commissions, any fees related to the sale and what the expected seller profit is to be.

Chapter 7: Moving Forward to New Adventures

Part One: Reflecting On The Journey

The Dallas-Fort Worth Metroplex has always been synonymous with luxury, where sprawling estates and opulent homes stand as monuments to the dreams and aspirations of those fortunate enough to call this vibrant region home. As a real estate agent specializing in luxury properties, I have the privilege of working with clients who sought to turn these dreams into reality.

Selling a luxury home in this area is not just a transaction; it's an art form, a ballet of negotiation, marketing, and showcasing the unparalleled qualities of a property. It's a journey filled with challenges and exhilarating moments that eventually lead to the ultimate goal: the sale of a prestigious home.

To begin, the process of selling a luxury home requires a a sharp eye for design and presentation, and an unwavering commitment to exceptional customer service. In the Dallas area, luxury homes are not just pieces of real estate; they are art. They have personality and history, reflecting the distinctive tastes and stories of their owners. My role is to honor that legacy and ensure the property shows like a diamond in a vast sea of properties.

Once the sale is complete, the journey doesn't end; it takes on a new form. The real estate market in the Dallas area is a world of its own, with a community of owners who share a passion for extraordinary living. As I reflected on my journey with clients after the sale, I realized that I had become not just their real estate agent but also a part of their story.

The bonds formed during the process of selling a luxury home were something special. It was more than just business; it was a partnership built on trust, mutual respect, and shared dreams. I often received invitations to housewarming parties, and it was heartwarming to see the joy and satisfaction on the faces of my clients as they settled into their new homes.

Some clients even turned into friends, and we meet for dinners or social events. They would share stories of their new lives in their luxury homes, and I would be reminded of the part I had played in helping them achieve their dreams.

Selling homes is not just a job; it was a passion, a calling. It is about connecting people with the extraordinary, helping them find their place in the world of opulence and elegance. And as I look back on my journey in this industry, I can't help but feel a profound sense of fulfillment. Each sale is not just a transaction; it was a chapter in the larger story of the Dallas real estate market, and I am grateful to be a part of it.

Part Two: Looking Ahead to New Beginnings

After the exhilarating experience of successfully selling your luxury market home, it's time to shift your focus towards the next chapter in your life. The sale of your property signifies not only a financial achievement but also the opportunity for a fresh start. This pivotal moment calls for careful consideration and planning as you embark on your journey towards a new beginning.

Reflect on Your Goals

Before rushing into your next venture, it's essential to take some time for introspection. Reflect on your long-term and short-term goals, both personal and professional. What is it that you want to accomplish in the next few years? Whether it's a career change, a new city, or simply a change in lifestyle, your goals will shape your path forward.

Financial Planning

With the proceeds from the sale of your luxury home, you'll have a significant financial foundation to build upon. Consult with financial experts to develop a comprehensive financial plan. This plan should address investment strategies, tax considerations, and a budget for your future endeavors.

Find Your Next Home

Once you've determined your goals and assessed your financial situation, it's time to find your next home, or this could be something you've already done prior to selling your existing home. Whether it's another luxurious property, a downsized apartment, or a charming countryside retreat, carefully consider what kind of living space will support your new chapter.

Explore New Experiences

Selling a luxury home is often a life-altering event. Use this as an opportunity to explore new experiences and possibilities. Perhaps it's time to travel, learn a new skill, or engage in philanthropic pursuits. The world is full of opportunities, and your luxury home sale has provided you with the means to embrace them.

Reinvent Your Lifestyle

A new beginning is a chance to reinvent your lifestyle. Consider what aspects of your daily routine you'd like to change or improve. This could involve health and fitness, social relationships, or personal hobbies. With your luxury property sold, you have the freedom to design a lifestyle that aligns with your aspirations.

Part Three: Resources for Ongoing Support

Build a Support Network

Embracing a new beginning can be both exciting and challenging. Surround yourself with a support network that includes family, friends, and possibly a life coach or counselor. They can provide guidance, encouragement, and perspective as you navigate this transformative phase of your life.

Give Back

Consider using some of the proceeds from your luxury home sale to give back to the community or causes you care about. Philanthropy can be a fulfilling way to leave a lasting impact and create a sense of purpose in your new beginning.

Personal Growth

Focus on personal growth and self-improvement. Continue to learn, grow, and evolve as an individual. This might include taking up new hobbies, attending workshops, or pursuing education that aligns with your interests and aspirations.

Stay Connected

While you may be leaving behind your luxury market home, it's important to stay connected with the friends and neighbors you've known. These connections can provide a sense of continuity and support as you transition into your new life.

Embrace Change

Lastly, remember that change is a natural part of life. Embrace it with an open heart and a positive mindset. The sale of your luxury home represents a new beginning, an opportunity to reinvent yourself and explore uncharted territory. Stay open to the possibilities that lie ahead and have confidence in your ability to create a bright future.

In this new chapter of your life, you have the chance to shape your destiny and embark on an exciting journey. The sale of your luxury market home is merely the beginning of a new adventure, full of potential and opportunity. Embrace it with enthusiasm, and remember that the canvas of your life is now open to paint the masterpiece of your dreams.

Selling Your Luxury Home Checklist

Selling a luxury home is a significant undertaking that requires careful planning, attention to detail, and a strategic approach. In this chapter, we will provide you with a comprehensive checklist to ensure a successful and profitable sale of your luxury property. Whether you're an experienced real estate investor or a first-time seller, this checklist will help you navigate the complex world of luxury real estate.

Part One: Preparing Your Luxury Home

1.1 Home Staging

Clean, declutter, and depersonalize your home to create a blank canvas for potential buyers.

Invest in professional staging services to showcase your home's potential.

Address any necessary repairs, painting, or renovations to make your home look its best.

1.2 Professional Photography and Videography

Hire a skilled photographer and videographer who specialize in luxury properties to capture the essence of your home.

Ensure that the photos and videos are taken during the best lighting conditions to showcase your home in its optimal state.

1.3 Appraisal and Pricing Strategy

Obtain a current appraisal of your property to understand its market value.

Work with a real estate agent to determine an accurate, competitive asking price.

Consider pricing strategies such as setting the price slightly higher to leave room for negotiation.

1.4 Curb Appeal

Enhance the exterior of your home with landscaping and exterior maintenance.

Invest in high-quality outdoor lighting and consider professional landscaping services.

2.1 Luxury Real Estate Agent

Choose a reputable real estate agent with experience in the luxury market.

Review their marketing plan, track record, and network within the luxury real estate community.

2.2 Online Presence

Develop a compelling online listing for your luxury property with professional photos and a detailed description.

Use high-end platforms and websites to target luxury buyers.

2.3 Social Media Marketing

Promote your home on various social media platforms, including Instagram, Facebook, and LinkedIn.

Utilize targeted advertising to reach affluent buyers.

2.4 Luxury Brochures and Marketing Materials

Design elegant brochures and promotional materials that showcase your home's unique features.

Highlight the lifestyle and exclusivity that your property offers.

2.5 Networking

Leverage your real estate agent's extensive network to connect with luxury buyers and other agents.

Attend luxury real estate events and open houses to expand your reach.

Part Three: Showings & Open Houses

3.1 Private Showings

Schedule private showings to allow potential buyers to experience the property without distractions.

Ensure your home is immaculately clean and well-maintained for each showing.

3.2 Open Houses

Host exclusive open houses for serious buyers and select guests.

Offer refreshments and engage with visitors to create a welcoming atmosphere.

3.3 Home Inspections

Be prepared for home inspections and provide necessary documentation regarding your property's condition.

Address any potential issues before they become deal-breakers.

Part Four: Negotiation & Closing

4.1 Offers and Negotiation

Review offers carefully with your real estate agent and consider your options.

Be prepared to negotiate terms such as price, contingencies, and closing dates.

4.2 Legal and Financial Guidance

Consult with an attorney and financial advisor to ensure all legal and financial aspects of the sale are in order.

Understand tax implications and consider 1031 exchanges or other strategies to minimize tax liability.

4.3 Final Walk-Through

Accommodate a final walk-through for the buyer to ensure the property is in the agreed-upon condition.

4.4 Closing Process

Work closely with your real estate agent and legal team to complete the closing process efficiently.

Transfer ownership and keys to the new owner.

Part Five: Post-Sale Considerations

5.1 Transition Planning

Plan for your own transition, whether it's to a new home or another investment.

Coordinate with movers and service providers as needed.

5.2 Closing Out Utilities and Services

Notify utility companies, service providers, and local authorities of the sale to avoid any unnecessary bills.

5.3 Thank-You Notes and Feedback

Consider sending thank-you notes to everyone involved in the sale, including the buyers and their agents.

Request feedback from your real estate agent to improve your future selling strategies.

Selling a luxury home can be a rewarding endeavor, both financially and emotionally. By following this comprehensive checklist and working with a qualified real estate professional, you can maximize your chances of a successful sale and a smooth transition to your next venture.

Glossary of Real Estate Terms

In the world of luxury real estate, the vocabulary used to describe and transact high-end properties is both specialized and complex. As a luxury home seller, it's essential to understand the terminology commonly used in the industry to effectively navigate the process and communicate with potential buyers, real estate agents, and other professionals involved in the transaction. This glossary is a comprehensive guide to the key terms and phrases you may encounter when selling a luxury home.

Appraisal: The process of determining the fair market value of a luxury property. Appraisals are typically conducted by certified appraisers and play a crucial role in setting the listing price and securing financing for potential buyers.

As-Is: An indication that the luxury property is being sold in its current condition, without any warranties or guarantees for repairs or improvements. This term is common in luxury real estate transactions due to the high value and unique features of these homes.

Brokerage: A real estate company or agency that provides services to buyers and sellers. Luxury homes often require specialized brokerages with expertise in high-end properties.

Comparative Market Analysis (CMA): An analysis prepared by a real estate agent that assesses the value of a luxury property by comparing it to similar properties in the area. This helps determine the appropriate listing price.

Contingency: A condition included in a real estate contract that must be met for the sale to proceed. Common contingencies in luxury home sales include financing, inspections, and appraisals.

Listing Agreement: A contract between a luxury home seller and a real estate agent or brokerage outlining the terms and conditions of the sale, including the listing price, commission, and marketing strategy.

Escrow: An account, typically held by a neutral third party, where funds are deposited during the sale process. These funds are released when the conditions of the sale are met.

Staging: The process of preparing a luxury home for sale by enhancing its appearance and appeal. Staging involves arranging furniture, decor, and lighting to showcase the property's best features.

Open House: An event where prospective buyers can tour a luxury home that's for sale. Open houses are an important part of marketing high-end properties to a broad audience.

Pocket Listing: A luxury property that is not publicly listed on the Multiple Listing Service (MLS). It is often marketed privately to a select group of potential buyers and agents, adding an element of exclusivity.

Seller's Disclosure: A document in which the luxury home seller provides information about the property's condition and any known issues. This is a legal requirement in many jurisdictions to protect buyers.

Title Insurance: A policy that protects the luxury home buyer and lender from any disputes over the property's ownership or title. It ensures that the property's title is clear and free of any liens or encumbrances.

Negotiation: The process of discussing and reaching an agreement on the terms and price of the luxury home sale. Effective negotiation is crucial in achieving a successful transaction.

Due Diligence: The comprehensive research and investigation conducted by the buyer and their team to verify the property's condition, legal status, and suitability. This includes inspections, appraisal, and legal reviews.

Concierge Services: Exclusive services offered by luxury real estate agents and brokerages to cater to the unique needs and desires of high-end clients, such as access to private showings, luxury transportation, and introductions to top-tier service providers.

Covenants, Conditions, and Restrictions (CC&Rs): Rules and regulations that govern the use of a luxury property located within a community or homeowners' association. Buyers need to be aware of these before purchasing.

Private Residence Club: A luxury property ownership structure where multiple individuals share ownership of a high-end property and have access to it for a specified period each year. These are often found in luxury resort areas.

Smart Home: A luxury property equipped with advanced automation and control systems, allowing the owner to manage security, lighting, climate, and entertainment with ease.

Walk-Through: A final inspection of the luxury property conducted by the buyer before closing to ensure that it is in the agreed-upon condition and any agreed-upon repairs or changes have been made.

This glossary provides a foundation for understanding the language of luxury real estate, but it is by no means exhaustive. Luxury home sales often involve unique and custom features that may require additional terminology and expertise. To ensure a smooth and successful transaction, consider working with a real estate professional experienced in luxury properties who can guide you through the process and help you navigate the intricacies of this specialized market.

Kim Meli Lovett

Kim is passionate about being a realtor. She also has an extensive background in marketing which supplies her with a toolbox full of innovative and creative ideas to effectively market homes for her sellers.

When not out and about working hard for her clients, she enjoys spending time with her husband Kirk, daughter Madison and son in law, Justin...as well as with her three adorable dogs!

To book a consultation or find out more about Kim visit www.KimLovettRealtor.com. To hear local market news and updates tune into her weekly show at www.MarketMovesDFW.com.

Made in the USA
Monee, IL
04 November 2026

67375750R00079